PRAIRIE DOGS
Tunnel Diggers

Lynn George

PowerKiDS
press
New York

Published in 2011 by The Rosen Publishing Group, Inc.
29 East 21st Street, New York, NY 10010

Copyright © 2011 by The Rosen Publishing Group, Inc.

First Edition

Editor: Joanne Randolph
Book Design: Kate Laczynski
Photo Researcher: Jessica Gerweck

Photo Credits: Cover, p. 1 © www.iStockphoto.com/Jessica Fries; back cover and interior blueprint © www.iStockphoto.com/Branko Miokovic; pp. 4 (left), 6, 8, 14 (prairie dog), 16, 21 Shutterstock.com; p. 4 (right) © www.iStockphoto.com/Henk Bentlage; p. 5 © www.iStockphoto.com/Mark Lundborg; p. 7 © Michael Krabs/age fotostock; p. 9 © www.iStockphoto.com/Roberto A. Sanchez; p. 10 Frank Greenaway/Getty Images; p. 11 De Agostini/Getty Images; p. 12 Gary Vestal/Getty Images; p. 13 © John Shaw/age fotostock; p. 14 (hard hat) © www.iStockphoto.com/Charles Shapiro; pp. 14–15 Jeff Foott/Getty Images; p. 17 G. Richard Kettlewell/Getty Images; pp. 18–19 All Canada Photos/SuperStock; p. 20 Ronald Wittek/Getty Images; p. 22 © www.iStockphoto.com/Roman Kobzarev.

Library of Congress Cataloging-in-Publication Data

George, Lynn.
  Prairie dogs : tunnel diggers / Lynn George. — 1st ed.
      p. cm. — (Animal architects)
  Includes index.
  ISBN 978-1-4488-0695-9 (library binding) — ISBN 978-1-4488-1351-3 (pbk.) —
ISBN 978-1-4488-1352-0 (6-pack)
  1. Prairie dogs—Juvenile literature. I. Title.
  QL737.R68G46 2011
  599.36'7—dc22
                              2010008867

Manufactured in the United States of America

CPSIA Compliance Information: Batch #WS10PK: For Further Information contact Rosen Publishing, New York, New York at 1-800-237-9932

CONTENTS

MEET THE PRAIRIE DOG

Prairie dogs often come out of their tunnels to warm themselves up in the sun, as this one here is doing.

This prairie dog is checking for enemies. If it sees one, it will start barking to tell the others about the danger.

Have you ever heard of a **prairie** dog? Its name might make you think it is a dog that lives on the prairie. This is partly true. It does live on the prairie, but it is not a dog. It is part of the squirrel family. It is called a prairie dog because it makes a barking sound.

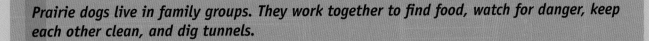

These lively animals look like large squirrels with short, furry tails. They have light brown fur, small eyes and ears, short legs, and long, sharp claws. They are generally 14 to 17 inches (36–43 cm) long, including their tails. They weigh between 1 and 3 pounds (0.5–1.5 kg).

Prairie dogs are known for being animal **architects**. They build huge **systems** of tunnels that connect to one another.

5

LOTS OF PRAIRIE DOGS

There are five kinds of prairie dogs. Two kinds live in low grasslands. Black-tailed prairie dogs are the largest and most common type of prairie dog. Mexican prairie dogs are **rare**. Both of these kinds have black-tipped tails. Mexican prairie dogs also have touches of black throughout their fur.

Take a look at this prairie dog's tail and see if you can guess what kind it is. If you guessed that it is a black-tailed prairie dog, then you were right!

The other three types live in high deserts and mountain valleys. White-tailed prairie dogs have white-tipped tails. Gunnison's prairie dogs have dark heads and gray-tipped tails. Utah prairie dogs

are the smallest kind of prairie dog. They have white tails and dark spots above and below their eyes. Most prairie dogs live in the western parts of North America.

A PRAIRIE DOG DAY

Above: *Here two prairie dogs greet each other.* Right: *Prairie dogs like to eat grass the best, but they also eats roots, seeds, and sometimes bugs.*

What do you do during the day? Maybe you eat, visit with friends and family, and clean your room. Prairie dogs do those things, too! Just as people are, prairie dogs are **social** animals. They live in groups, and they have jobs to do in their **community**.

Prairie dogs live in tunnels, called burrows. During the day, they mend and clean their burrows. Outside, they eat plants and bugs. They spend time together. Prairie dogs often greet each other by touching their front teeth together. Adults **groom** each other, and young prairie dogs

play. Some prairie dogs watch for danger and bark when enemies approach. Their barks tell other prairie dogs important facts about these enemies, such as how fast they are coming. If needed, prairie dogs dive into their burrows for safety.

9

Did you know that prairie dog homes have different rooms for different purposes, just as your home does? They even have front doors and back doors. Prairie dog tunnels are planned communities.

Prairie dogs use their long, sharp claws to dig their

Here a prairie dog is starting to dig a new tunnel. **Facing page:** *This drawing shows how a prairie dog tunnel might look. Do you see the different rooms and the mounds by the openings?*

burrows. They dig long tunnels. They make several entrances so they have ways to escape if an enemy comes through one opening. Listening post rooms are just inside the entrances so prairie dogs can listen for danger outside. Deeper inside are sleeping rooms and **nursery** burrows. They even have separate rooms for toilets! They clean these rooms out from time to time.

IN THE NURSERY

One special room in a prairie dog tunnel is called the nursery burrow. This room is there specially for raising young prairie dogs. Young prairie dogs are called pups. About three to five pups are born in spring or early summer. When the mother is ready to have her pups, she goes to the nursery burrow. The pups are

A baby prairie dog greets its mother. Prairie dogs can be very loving with their families. Facing page: A mother and a baby prairie dog take a rest together.

born with their eyes closed, and they have no fur. Their mother feeds them milk from her body and **protects** them. The pups begin to go outside and eat grass when they are about six weeks old.

After about a year, the males move away. The females stay nearby. Both the males and females look for **mates**. Then they dig their own tunnels and have their own pups!

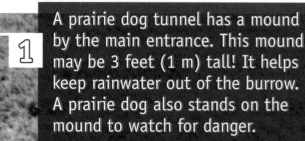

INSIDE VIEW: *PRAIRIE DOG TUNNELS*

1 A prairie dog tunnel has a mound by the main entrance. This mound may be 3 feet (1 m) tall! It helps keep rainwater out of the burrow. A prairie dog also stands on the mound to watch for danger.

The second entrance, or back door, has a smaller mound. It is generally about 1 foot (30 cm) tall. Wind blows fresh air into the burrow through this opening.

8

A burrow even has a special room used as a bathroom or toilet. Prairie dogs clean out this room from time to time.

7

Storage rooms hold seeds and other food. That way, prairie dogs can still eat when weather forces them to stay in their burrows.

6

2 A listening post room is just inside the entrance, right below the surface of the ground. Here, a prairie dog can stay safely hidden and still hear if enemies are outside.

3 The tunnel goes down for 3 to 16 feet (1–5 m). Then it becomes level and runs for 13 to 110 feet (4–34 m).

5 The nursery burrow has a nest of dried grass and leaves, too. It is big enough for the mother and all her babies to be comfortable for six weeks.

4 The sleeping rooms have nests of dried grass and leaves. These rooms are higher than the bottom of the burrow so they stay dry if water gets inside.

ONE BIG, HAPPY FAMILY

Just like people, prairie dogs live with their families. Most prairie dog families are made up of a male, three or four females, and their young. This family group is called a **coterie**.

Each coterie has its own **territory**. The territory covers about 1 acre (.4 ha) and has about 60 burrow entrances.

There can be up to 35 prairie dogs in a coterie. Male babies will leave to form their own coteries once they can live on their own.

Mother prairie dogs generally give birth to four or five babies at one time. They feed their babies for about six weeks.

Coterie members share almost everything. They work together to raise their young and guard their territory. They groom one another and play together. They share the burrows and the food. The only time this is not true is when there are new babies. Then the mother will not let anyone else in the nursery burrow.

PRAIRIE DOG TOWNS

Does your family live in a neighborhood? Prairie dog families live in neighborhoods, too! There may be many family groups living side by side in neighborhoods. Several neighborhoods make up a town, just as they do for people.

Prairie dogs in a town sometimes fight. Each coterie guards its territory from others. They do not want other prairie dogs in

their burrows. You might wonder, then, why prairie dogs form towns? It is safer to live in big groups. More eyes can look for danger.

A prairie dog town generally covers about 247 acres (100 ha), or .4 square mile (1 sq km), and has thousands of prairie dogs. The largest town ever found was 25,000 square miles (65,000 sq km) and had 400 million prairie dogs!

EMPTY BURROWS, NEW HOMES

Do you know what a ghost town is? It is a town that has been **abandoned** and remains empty. Sometimes prairie dogs have to abandon their town, too. However, their abandoned towns do not remain empty for long.

Many animals make homes in the abandoned burrows. These include

Foxes (above) and rabbits (facing page) are two kinds of animals that are happy to take over abandoned prairie dog burrows.

burrowing owls, rattlesnakes, tiger **salamanders**, rabbits, badgers, foxes, weasels, black-footed ferrets, and even bugs.

Snakes, burrowing owls, and black-footed ferrets sometimes even move in while prairie dogs are still living in their burrows. That can be bad news for the prairie dogs since snakes and ferrets like to eat them!

PROTECTING PRAIRIE DOGS

Did you know that prairie dogs are important to all prairie life? Their architecture makes the soil better. Their tunnels allow more water into the soil. Their waste makes it richer. Plants grow better because of these things. Many animals come to the prairie to eat the plentiful plants.

Other animals come to eat the prairie dogs. The wonderful tunnels prairie dogs build become homes for many animals.

Sadly, prairie dogs are disappearing. People wrongly think prairie dogs are pests and kill them. People are also destroying or hurting the places prairie dogs need to build their homes. Today, some people are working to protect prairie dogs. How can you help?

GLOSSARY

abandoned (uh-BAN-dund) Left without planning to come back.

architects (AHR-kuh-tekts) People who create ideas and plans for a building.

community (kuh-MYOO-nih-tee) A place where people or animals live and work together or the people or animals who make up such a place.

coterie (KOHT-uh-ree) A small group of animals that often come together socially.

groom (GROOM) To clean someone's body and make it neat.

mates (MAYTS) Male and female animals that come together to make babies.

nursery (NURS-ree) A place where babies are cared for.

prairie (PRER-ee) A large place with flat land and grass but few or no trees.

protects (pruh-TEKTS) Keeps safe.

rare (RER) Not common.

salamanders (SA-luh-man-durz) Animals that look like lizards but that live and breathe underwater when young and do not have scaly skin.

social (SOH-shul) Living together in a group.

systems (SIS-temz) Many different parts that work together as a whole.

territory (TER-uh-tor-ee) Land or space that is guarded by an animal for its use.

INDEX

WEB SITES

Due to the changing nature of Internet links, PowerKids Press has developed an online list of Web sites related to the subject of this book. This site is updated regularly. Please use this link to access the list:

www.powerkidslinks.com/arch/prairdog/